MYLES MUNROE
ON LEADERSHIP

INPIRATIONAL INSIGHTS FOR THE FRONTLINE LEADER

Pneuma Life

PUBLISHING

MYLES MUNROE ON LEADERSHIP

ON LEADERSHIP

INPIRATIONAL INSIGHTS FOR THE FRONTLINE LEADER

MYLES MUNROE ON LEADERSHIP

Printed in the United States of America

Copyright © 1997 - Myles Munroe
Dr. Myles Munroe
P.O. Box N-9583
Nassau, Bahamas

Myles Munroe on Leadership   ISBN 1-56229-115-7

Pneuma Life Publishing
P. O. Box 885
Lanham, Maryland 20703-0885
(301) 577-4052
http://www.pneumalife.com

Introduction

The world is filled with followers, supervisors, and managers but very few leaders. Leadership is like beauty, it's hard to define but you know it when you see it. Time has produced a legacy of distinguished and outstanding individuals who have impacted history and the ongoing development of mankind. These people were both men and women, rich and poor, learned and unlearned, trained and untrained. They came from every race, color, language and culture of the world. Many of them had no ambition to become great or renowned. They were simple people who were victims of circumstances that demanded the hidden qualities of their character, or they were driven by a personal passionate goal.

It is in this environment that we, as stewards of this present age, must face the challenge of identifying, developing, training, releasing and reproducing a generation of leaders who would secure the future for our children and their children. This inspirational book is designed to contribute to this challenge. It is my hope that you would be inspired to respond to the call of destiny and responsibility, and maximize the leadership potential within you.

A good leader not only knows where he is going, but he can inspire others to go with him.

A true leader is a model for his followers.

Great leaders never
desire to lead but to serve.

Leadership has very little to do with what you do and is fundamentally a matter of becoming who you are.

Leaders are simply people who dare to be themselves and are able to express themselves fully.

You become a leader when you decide
not to be a copy but an original.

We are all capable of leadership by design, but we cannot lead correctly and effectively unless we are led by His Spirit.

Leadership is the ability of one person to influence others.

Leadership is first being, then doing.

A title and position do not guarantee
performance and productivity.

Leadership is impossible without a guiding vision and a purpose that generates passion for accomplishment.

The purest form of leadership is influence through inspiration.

Inspiration is the opposite of intimidation and is absent of manipulation.

An important ingredient of the leadership function is the ability to draw the best out of other people.

Real qualities of leadership are to be found in those who are willing to suffer for the sake of objectives great enough to demand their whole-hearted obedience.

Good leaders employ others, great leaders deploy themselves and others.

You were born to lead but you must become a leader, just as one may be born a male but must become a man.

A leader is one who leads
others to leadership.

The essence of becoming a leader
is knowing and becoming yourself.

True leaders learn from others, but they are not made by nor become others.

Leaders are more concerned
with expressing themselves, than
with proving themselves.

True leaders do not try to be; they just are.

Regardless of title, you cannot be
a leader without followers.

True leaders are inwardly directed, self assured, and, as a result, truly charismatic.

True success is the fulfillment of original purpose.

Effectiveness is not doing things right, but doing the right things.

You possess the capacity to be
a leader within the sphere of the
purpose for which you were born.

Leaders are individuals who
have declared independence
from the expectations of others.

The purpose for leadership is to inspire every follower to become a leader and fulfill his potential.

True leadership brings followers
into leadership and makes
itself increasingly unnecessary.

You are a successful leader when
your followers can lead others.

True leadership provides
opportunity for others to find
and fulfill their God-given purpose.

The purpose for leadership is not
the maintenance of followers,
but the production of leaders.

Success without a successor is failure.

The greatest display
of leadership is service.

Leadership is born out of
character and determination.

A leader is simply a person
who has a sphere of influence.

One is not qualified to give orders until he can receive them.

If you are going to be an effective
leader, you must be prepared.

You should be motivated by your love for people, not by your desire to be great.

Authority does not make you a leader;
it gives you the opportunity to be one.

Inspiration is the key to true leadership.

True leadership is not something you grasp but something you become.

Genuine leadership is a marriage
of the natural and spiritual qualities
producing a well integrated character.

As a leader, you cannot drive
people; you must lead them.

Leaders don't draw
attention to themselves.

Great leaders are ordinary people who did extraordinary things because circumstances made demands on their potential.

Leaders learn from others, but they are not made by others.

To be an effective leader, you may listen to all, but in the end, be responsible for your own decisions.

All leaders are the targets of criticism.

A good leader does not depend on
people's opinions to confirm
God's will for his life.

57

You cannot fully conquer kingdoms until you have conquered yourself.

When people have confidence in your
leadership, your work will prosper.

If you can inspire, you can mobilize.

True leaders are not afraid to establish
strong friendships because they
are secure in themselves.

You cannot really help people
if you don't like them.

It's very difficult to be a representative
of God if you are prejudiced.

A good leader knows how to love people just as they are.

True leaders know who they are, and the authority under which they function.

Until you are willing to die for
what you are living for, you
cannot become a true leader.

A good leader remains optimistic.

True leaders are not annoyed by people's failures, they are challenged by them.

Failure is a temporary detour and should never become a permanent address.

As in every seed there is a forest, so in every follower there is a leader.

The quality of your character is the measure of your leadership effectiveness.

True leadership cannot be divorced
from the basic qualities that
produce good sound character.

Leaders are not born,
but are created by life.

A leader must have a proper estimation of himself in Christ Jesus.

Maturity is indispensable
to good leadership.

75

All great leaders are products of
time and trophies of life's wars.

True leaders initiate their own learning.

Great leaders love knowledge;
they always want to know.

To a leader, the family will not
be sacrificed for anything.

A leader must be found
faithful in stewardship.

Real leadership power comes
from an honorable character.

A leader must have wisdom.

Effective leadership is the perfect balance of competence, vision and virtue.

A leader should be above reproach.

The character of a leader should
be one that commands respect
from all, even his enemies.

A leader must allow himself no indulgence in secrets that would undermine his character or mar his public witness.

A leader must be a gentle person.

If you desire to be a leader, be willing to gain experience over time and understand that you have to qualify for the trust and confidence of others.

A leader is somebody who could see beyond what everybody else was looking at.

When you have tasted possibilities, it is very difficult to settle for impossibilities.

Wisdom is the ability to make
use of knowledge effectively.

Courage is resistance to and mastery of fear, not the absence of fear.

True leaders are naturally humble.

Humility is the ability to control power.

The leader should not be
motivated by, or greedy for money.

Humility is knowing who you are and accepting it without boasting.

A true leader hates the things God hates.

Leaders possess the faculty of being able to attract and draw the best out of other people.

The man who is impatient with weakness
will be defective in his leadership.

Leaders are men of faith, for faith is vision.

A leader must be able to reconcile opposing viewpoints without giving offense and without compromising principle.

If you are ready for criticism,
you're ready for leadership.

True character is made in
secret and is displayed openly.

Leadership demands a commitment of service to others, a placing of the needs of others above our own.

Criticism is the leader's greatest test of maturity, conviction and commitment to his vision.

If you are not willing to stand alone
in your vision, not many will be
willing to stand with you.

It is better to be criticized for action
than to be ignored for non-action.

Leadership is lonely, because to lead means you must be out in front, ahead of the followers.

All leaders must possess an
exceptional degree of stamina
and physical energy if they are to
effectively motivate and inspire others.

If you are willing to pay the price of fatigue, then you are willing to lead.

No true leader can expect to live
a normal life as other people do.

Leaders belong to their
generation and not to themselves.

True leaders cultivate character
with the fertilizer of self discipline.

If you do not want to be criticized,
then decide to do nothing in life.

True leaders possess the horizon
perspective and a frontier spirit.

A leader who knows who he is
does not depend on others to
validate his sense of self-worth.

Pride is usually evidence of a poor self-concept and low self-esteem.

True leaders never forget from whence they came, and live to bring others to where they are.

One of the greatest dangers to leaders is the temptation to measure all others by oneself.

Egotism is a manifestation
of pride and insecurity.

True leaders are always aware that they are only a link in a long, historical chain.

The true leader does not measure his success by comparing himself with others, but with his own purpose and vision.

If you are sure of your own assignment in life, then you are free from competition, comparison and thus, jealousy.

The greatest and most common peril of leadership is that of disqualifying oneself from the position of leadership.

Leaders see the world
while others see the village.

The quality of tomorrow's leaders lies
in the character of today's followers.

Success is not measured by what a man accomplishes, but by the opposition he has encountered, and the courage with which he has maintained the struggle against overwhelming odds.

The measure of a man is the way he bears up under misfortune.

To win without risk is to
triumph without glory.

He who would accomplish little must sacrifice little; he who would achieve much must sacrifice much.

The time to repair the roof
is when the sun is shining.

If we do what is necessary, all
the odds are in our favor.

Our attitude is not determined
by circumstances, but by how
we respond to circumstances.

What happens to a man is less significant than what happens within him.

I've never been poor, only broke.
Being poor is a frame of mind. Being
broke is only a temporary situation.

The good or bad is not in the
circumstance, but only in the
mind of him that encounters it.

Things turn out best for the people who
make the best of the way things turn out.

The men who try to do something
and fail are infinitely better than those
who try to do nothing and succeed.

The man who makes no mistakes
does not usually make anything.

To win, you've got to stay in the game.

All things are possible
for him who believes.

There is no law by which one
can as long as he thinks he can't.

Our greatest power is
the power to choose.

The thoughts we have chosen have brought us where we are today.

As I grow older, I pay less attention to what men say. I just watch what they do.

The actions of men are the best
interpreters of their thoughts.

Seeing success where others see
only failure may be the one thing
that pushes us on to victory.

In every adversity there lies the seed of an equivalent advantage. In every defeat there is a lesson showing you how to win the victory next time.

The hopeful man sees success where others see failure, sunshine where others see shadows and storm.

One has to remember that every
failure can be a stepping-stone
to something better.

Singleness of purpose is one of the
chief essentials for success in life,
no matter what may be one's aim.

Concentrate; put all your eggs in one basket, and watch that basket.

The secret to becoming
confident is preparation.

There can be no great courage where there is no confidence or assurance, and half the battle is in the conviction that we can do what we undertake.

It generally happens that assurance
keeps an even pace with ability.

The most dramatic conflicts are perhaps, those that take place not between men but between a man and himself where the arena of conflict is a solitary mind.

To be conscious that you are
ignorant is the first step to knowledge.

Other Books by Dr. Myles Munroe

Becoming A Leader
Becoming A Leader Workbook
Seasons of Change
Understanding Your Potential
Releasing Your Potential
Maximizing Your Potential
In Pursuit of Purpose
Potent Quotes